Thurgood Marshall and *Brown v. Board of Education of Topeka*

Zachary Deibel

 Cavendish
Square

New York

Dedication: To my mother.

"None of us got where we are solely by pulling ourselves up by our bootstraps. We got here because somebody—a parent, a teacher—bent down and helped us pick up our boots."
—Justice Thurgood Marshall

Published in 2017 by Cavendish Square Publishing, LLC
243 5th Avenue, Suite 136, New York, NY 10016

Copyright © 2017 by Cavendish Square Publishing, LLC

First Edition

Library of Congress Cataloging-in-Publication Data

Names: Deibel, Zachary, author.
Title: Thurgood Marshall and Brown v. Board of Education / Zachary Deibel.
Description: New York: Cavendish Square Publishing, 2016. | Series: Primary sources of the civil rights movement | Includes bibliographical references and index. | Description based on print version record and CIP data provided by publisher; resource not viewed. Identifiers: LCCN 2015048470 (print) | LCCN 2015048095 (ebook) | ISBN 9781502618672 (ebook) | ISBN 9781502618665 (library bound)
Subjects: LCSH: Marshall, Thurgood, 1908-1993. | Judges--United States—Biography. | United States. Supreme Court—Biography. | Brown, Oliver, 1918-1961—Trials, litigation, etc. | Topeka (Kan.). Board of Education—Trials, litigation, etc. | Segregation in education—Law and legislation—United States. | Discrimination in education—Law and legislation—United States. | African Americans—Civil rights. Classification: LCC KF8745.M34 (print) | LCC KF8745.M34 D45 2016 (ebook) | DDC 344.73/0798—dc23
LC record available at http://lccn.loc.gov/2015048470

Editorial Director: David McNamara
Editor: Fletcher Doyle
Copy Editor: Nathan Heidelberger
Art Director: Jeffrey Talbot
Senior Designer: Amy Greenan
Production Assistant: Karol Szymczuk
Photo Researcher: J8 Media

Printed in the United States of America

CONTENTS

INTRODUCTION • 4
Precedent for Prejudice

CHAPTER ONE • 7
Mentor for Marshall

CHAPTER TWO • 18
No Equal Opportunity

CHAPTER THREE • 33
Position of Influence

CHAPTER FOUR • 44
Impact from the Bench

Chronology • 54

Glossary • 56

Further Information • 58

Bibliography • 60

Index • 62

About the Author • 64

Precedent for Prejudice

S tarting in the late 1800s, people and history combined to push large social, political, and economic changes on American society. World War I and World War II increased the influence of the United States on the rest of the world. The country's economy grew, particularly after the Great Depression, as business markets became global.

By the 1950s, the United States had expanded the rights of factory and farm workers; amended the Constitution to guarantee women's suffrage, which is the right to vote in national elections; and built organizations like the Social Security Administration to help the poor and the elderly. However, most of these efforts ignored a significant portion of the US population: African Americans.

Despite the result of the Civil War, African Americans continued to experience inequality, injustice, and oppression through the mid-1900s. After that war, Congress passed three "Reconstruction Amendments" to the United States Constitution. The Thirteenth Amendment ended slavery, the Fourteenth Amendment guaranteed citizenship and

Thurgood Marshall and *Brown v. Board of Education of Topeka*

equal protection under the law to all individuals born or naturalized in the United States, and the Fifteenth Amendment protected the right to vote for all male citizens, regardless of race. However, in the newly reunited South, many people and institutions remained resistant to these changes. They sought to undermine legal provisions for **equality** through **segregation**.

In 1896, Homer Plessy, a resident who was seven-eighths white and one-eighth black, sued Louisiana for racially segregating its railway system. The state required that seating and sleeping areas for black train passengers be separated from those for white passengers. In the majority opinion for the **Supreme Court of the United States**, Justice Henry Billings Brown argued that segregation was not, fundamentally, unconstitutional. Plessy's attorneys argued the policy violated both the Thirteenth and Fourteenth Amendments; the court asserted it did not. In its ruling in *Plessy v. Ferguson*, the court essentially legalized segregation—the enforced separation of society based on race.

Though the Supreme Court did not think "that the enforced separation of the two races stamp[ed] the colored race with a badge of inferiority," the Southern states used segregation to put African Americans at a disadvantage politically, socially, and economically. As a result of the ruling, nearly every state in the South passed laws segregating buses, trains, hotels, restaurants, movie theaters, and many other public and private institutions. Public schools became a key area in which Southern states aimed to enforce and enlarge segregation. Many states forbid the mixing of racial groups in education.

For nearly a century after the Civil War, Southern states used many legal precedents to justify segregation in schooling. At the same time, these states provided inferior education to black citizens. Reformers would see the true inequality that existed in Southern school systems.

African-American children clean the grounds of their school in 1896 after *Plessy v. Ferguson*. The resources given to these schools were far inferior to those provided to schools for white students.

However, the federal government ultimately did little to end these practices of segregation. In fact, theories of racial hierarchy dominated the period. Herbert Spencer argued other races were "subspecies" to those of white descent. Ideas like these revealed the intense racism of the period. From the end of the Civil War through the 1960s, African Americans faced legal disadvantages and oppression, all of which went against the promises of freedom after the Civil War. This was the reality for many Americans, a reality that prompted figures like Thurgood Marshall to push for equality under the law and an end to racism.

Thurgood Marshall and *Brown v. Board of Education of Topeka*

Mentor for Marshall

Through both legal and social segregation, African Americans faced incredible hardship throughout the early twentieth century. However, this oppression caused many to seek reform. Booker T. Washington, a young freedman, founded the Tuskegee Institute, which aimed to provide young African Americans with vocational training so they could earn a living as productive workers. Washington instructed blacks to "cast down your bucket where you are," advocating that African Americans remain in the South and work to be contributors to society. Washington argued, "In all things that are purely social," African Americans and white Americans "can be as separate as the fingers, yet one as the hand in all things essential to mutual progress." W. E. B. Du Bois, another reformer, argued for legal equality and education as the means through which blacks could secure true liberty. Du Bois criticized Washington's approach, suggesting, "Education

Civil rights activist W. E. B. Du Bois (*standing at right*) works in the offices of *Crisis,* a publication of the National Association for the Advancement of Colored People (NAACP). The photo was taken circa 1932.

must not simply teach work—it must teach life." Du Bois became the first African American to receive a PhD from Harvard University, and he maintained that a "talented tenth" of the African-American population could assist in advancing the political and social cause of equality.

Du Bois sought **integration**, a society that valued tolerance and inclusion, not separation and segregation. Du Bois founded the **National Association for the Advancement of Colored People** (NAACP) in 1909 to seek legal protection of black rights. Charles Hamilton Houston became an important leader of the organization as **legal counsel** in 1934, arguing several court cases that sought to desegregate public education throughout the period. Before starting his position with the NAACP, Houston was the first black editor of the *Harvard Law Review* and later served as vice-dean of Howard University's law school. Houston believed that "equality of educational opportunity [is] not an isolated struggle. All our

Thurgood Marshall and *Brown v. Board of Education of Topeka*

struggles must tie in together and support one another … We must remain on the alert and push the struggle farther with all our might." This idea drove Houston's work and his service at Howard University School of Law, where he mentored several lawyers until 1934, including a promising young student named Thurgood Marshall.

Thurgood Marshall was born in 1908 in Baltimore, Maryland, to Norma and William "Willie" Marshall. His parents taught him to pursue "a vision of blacks and whites living together as equals under the law." As part of the migration from the South to the North of many African Americans trying to get away from segregation, Marshall's family moved to Harlem in 1910. They stayed until 1914. While there, they witnessed the growing Harlem Renaissance. This was a period when artistic, literary, and intellectual expression created a new black culture. After his grandmother suffered an injury, the family returned to Baltimore, where Marshall spent the remainder of his adolescence.

Returning to live below the Mason–Dixon Line separating North from South, Marshall was again restrained by the racist institutions that surrounded him in post–Civil War America. Marshall commented in an interview, "There wasn't a single department store that would let a Negro in the front door." Citing "a study … made by the Urban League around 1930," Marshall explained, later in his life, "segregation in Baltimore was more rigid than any other county in this country, including Jackson, Mississippi." As a young man, Marshall worked as a delivery boy for a white storeowner named Mr. Schoen. In one encounter, Marshall recalled that a man shouted racial obscenities at him while he was boarding at the front of a trolley car on a delivery for Mr. Schoen. He was not aware that he had not followed the rules of racial segregation when he boarded. The man grabbed Marshall who, having been taught by his father to confront anyone who used particular obscenities that were insulting to all African Americans,

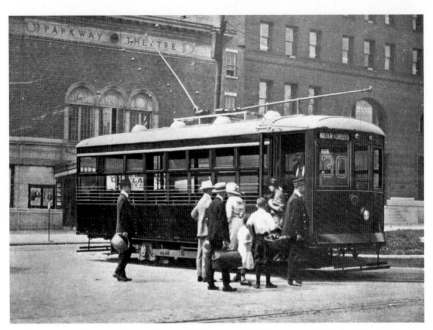

Trollies such as this safety car in Baltimore and other regions in the South were allowed to be segregated because of the Supreme Court's 1896 ruling that "separate but equal" facilities were constitutional.

proceeded to "have business with [him] then and there." After the altercation, Baltimore police arrested Marshall for assault.

That evening, Mr. Schoen's attorney's paid Marshall's bail, and he was able to negotiate Marshall's release. Marshall recalled Mr. Schoen's kindness as a moment that affirmed his belief in integration as a viable alternative to segregation. Marshall "apologized to him, because the five hats [he had been instructed to deliver] were wrecks and it was a complete loss to him, and he said, 'Forget about them, what about you?'" Encounters like these, where Marshall experienced oppression and injustice for the color of his skin, increased his commitment to **social justice**.

Marshall did not work hard in school until his mother, Norma, earned her college degree to become a teacher. He attended the segregated Frederick Douglass High School, where he combined promising academic performance with a "reputation as a cutup and prankster." As he neared college

Thurgood Marshall and *Brown v. Board of Education of Topeka*

age, Marshall worked as a porter for the Baltimore & Ohio Railroad. He eventually earned enough money to attend Lincoln University, a historically black college in southeastern Pennsylvania. While there, he became a prominent debater and law student. After completing his undergraduate degree, Marshall found himself a victim of discrimination yet again. In 1930, the University of Maryland Law School, his mother's dream school for her young son, refused to admit him based on his race. Instead, Marshall attended Howard University's law school, where the ambitious lawyer named Charles Hamilton Houston had recently been appointed vice-dean. Under Houston, Marshall applied his legal learning as a means "to dismantle the legal segregation that still disadvantaged African Americans." Marshall would later remember, "I don't know anything I did in the practice of law that wasn't the result of what Charlie Houston banged into my head."

One of the first cases Houston and Marshall took on together involved a black man accused of murdering two white women in Virginia. Houston was asked by Walter White, the head of the NAACP, to work on the case, and he gave Houston permission to use students to defend the man, George Crawford. They all feared Crawford would fall victim to a lynch mob, and Marshall threw himself into the work. White later wrote in his autobiography:

> There was a lanky, brash young senior law student who was always present. I used to wonder at his presence and sometimes was amazed at his assertiveness in challenging positions taken by Charlie and the other lawyers. But I soon learned of his great value ... [He did] everything he was asked, from research on obscure legal opinions to foraging for coffee and sandwiches. The law student was Thurgood Marshall ...

Marshall Challenged

While in college, Marshall began to consider the implications of defying segregation laws. In an interview with the Columbia Oral History Research Office in 1977, Marshall recalled a conversation with a law school peer: "I was telling him all these things that Negroes couldn't do [in Baltimore]. He says, 'How do you know it?' I said, 'Everybody knows it.' He said, 'Well, did you ever try?'"

Marshall said this moment "stuck in my craw, as to, why not do something about it?" This concept of defying unjust laws connected Marshall to early civil rights advocates. Marshall said his grandmother taught him to learn about the struggles for equality. He recalled, "I'd go and pull out books. The first one was Frederick Douglass, which incidentally I still read every once in a while—because I don't know of a Negro today, or later than Douglass, who had the courage he had, in the things he said."

The injustice he observed, combined with his scholarship and understanding of the fight for racial equality, shaped Marshall's dedication to civil rights.

Frederick Douglass was a central figure in Marshall's young intellectual life. The works of the famous abolitionist gave a vision to Marshall's legal career.

Thurgood Marshall and *Brown v. Board of Education of Topeka*

Even though the Howard University team could not secure an acquittal, they did avoid a death sentence for Crawford. By the end of Marshall's academic career, he had already learned the importance of civil rights reform and dedicated his life to promoting equality in America.

After graduation, Marshall opened his own law practice, accepting cases for African Americans who found themselves victims of an unjust system. As early as 1939, Marshall wrote on the importance of living up to the promise of the Fourteenth Amendment to the United States Constitution: equal protection under the law. In an article for the magazine *Crisis*, Marshall wrote about harsh realities of inequality in American society. Marshall commented:

> While it may be true that laws and constitutions do not act to right wrong and overturn established folkways overnight, it is also true that the reaffirmation of these principles of democracy build a body of public opinion in which rights and privileges of citizenship may be enjoyed, and in which the more brazen as well as the more sophisticated attempts at deprivation may be halted.

Marshall attacked segregation as a violation of the Constitution, one that states could not commit without also breaking federal law. In an article written with attorney William H. Hastie titled "Negro Discrimination and the Need for Federal Action," Marshall summarized his objectives as a lawyer plainly: "to obtain basic civil rights which have been denied [African Americans]" and "to protect such few rights as have heretofore been accorded them." These writings reflected Marshall's focus early in his career on segregation and civil rights law.

Thurgood Marshall works in his office as legal counsel to the NAACP.

In one of his early cases, Marshall experienced a horrible flaw in the judicial system. The parents of a young black man who had been arrested for murder in Southern Maryland wanted a black lawyer to represent their son. A neighbor convinced the parents to hire Marshall. He argued the man's innocence, as he was the driver of the criminal's car, not the attacker. The actual killer was represented by white attorneys, and received a life sentence. Marshall's client was hanged in 1935. Despite this setback, Marshall earned a good reputation for representing the hopeless. Marshall recalled one instance of an elderly black woman from North Carolina seeking legal counsel from Marshall, as he had been referred to her

Thurgood Marshall and *Brown v. Board of Education of Topeka*

Newspaper editor Carl Murphy presents an award to an ROTC member at Morgan State College after the military was desegregated in 1948.

as "a freebie lawyer," one who would take a case related to civil rights, even without compensation.

As his reputation grew, Marshall drew the attention of the NAACP, which looked for civil rights–minded attorneys. In 1934, Carl Murphy, editor of the *Afro-American* newspaper, asked Marshall to evaluate a series of proposed pieces of "innovative federal legislation that would empower Congress to define civil rights and invoke penalties for violations of those rights." Marshall looked at the issues in line with earlier civil rights cases that had been heard by the Supreme Court in the 1890s. He concluded that the fate of civil rights was in the hands of the courts, not in the legislature. He wrote in a letter to Murphy:

> In these cases, the Supreme Court laid down finally that it is not within the legislative power of Congress to define what are the civil rights of life, liberty and property of individuals and affix and enforce penalties for their denial by private persons.

As a result, the NAACP and other civil rights organizations soon asked for Marshall's expertise in seeking

Charles Hamilton Houston joined NAACP President Virginia McGuire at a protest in 1934.

legal reform. In one of his first cases for the NAACP, Marshall represented people who boycotted a business in his old neighborhood in west Baltimore. White Americans owned the business, which served both black and white

Thurgood Marshall and *Brown v. Board of Education of Topeka*

customers, but refused to hire black workers. In the case, Marshall collaborated with his old mentor, Charles Hamilton Houston. Houston argued "that blacks had a right to withhold their patronage from merchants who would not employ them." The NAACP won the case, setting a precedent for Marshall's work as a key legal advocate for equality within the organization. Marshall would continue advocating for reform as a means of securing equality, citing mob violence and **lynchings** that had plagued the South since Reconstruction. Marshall wrote in *Lawyers Guild Review*:

> Constitutional guarantees and laws guaranteeing civil rights are worthless scraps of paper to the people who are prevented from exercising these rights by the constant threat of mob violence … Only federal action will free us from lynchings and the threat of lynching.

For Marshall, the only reasonable solution to violent segregation and racism was nationwide action that would punish violators while settling the legality of the punishment.

It was at this time, in collaboration with Houston, that Marshall zeroed in on the case of *Plessy v. Ferguson* as the key hurdle to civic equality. Houston and Marshall began to formulate a legal strategy that contended the idea of "separate but equal" was, inherently, unequal. In 1934, the two lawyers traveled throughout the South to examine "the appalling state of black schools" as a means of undermining segregation that had been applied to the education system. The two attorneys worked tirelessly with the NAACP to find the appropriate legal foundation for a case that examined this exact issue.

CHAPTER TWO

No Equal Opportunity

In 1935, Charles Hamilton Houston and Thurgood Marshall found a case that would allow the NAACP to challenge school segregation. The University of Maryland's law school had rejected a young black student named Donald Gaines Murray. Interestingly, the same school had rejected Marshall's admission when he pursued a law degree. After being denied admission, Murray wrote to the university's president, Raymond A. Pearson. Pearson returned Murray's application and deposit, suggesting he ought to explore "the exceptional facilities open to you for the study of law at Howard University in Washington." Houston and Marshall used this rejection based on the student's race to destroy the practice of segregation at the University of Maryland and, fundamentally, throughout the nation.

Murray's own correspondence with the university aligned neatly with the legal strategy Houston and Marshall used. The applicant wrote:

Thurgood Marshall and *Brown v. Board of Education of Topeka*

A young Thurgood Marshall advises Donald Gaines Murray on his case against the University of Maryland.

I am a citizen of the State of Maryland and fully qualified to become a student at the University of Maryland Law School. No other State institution affords a legal education. The arbitrary action of the officials of the University of Maryland in returning my application was unjust and unreasonable and contrary to the Constitution and laws of the United States and the Constitution and laws of this State. I, therefore, appeal to you as the governing body of the University to accept the enclosed application …

Houston and Marshall aimed to prove that states did not provide equal educational institutions for both black and white Americans. In order to uphold the requirements of *Plessy v. Ferguson*, states must provide schools to black students of equal quality and opportunity. This would have proved an extensive cost to the states' legislatures. The Fourteenth Amendment to the Constitution further stressed the need for equal institutions. States were required to provide "equal protection of the laws," which extended to any state government. Therefore, Marshall and Houston hoped to force Maryland—and other states—to construct, finance, and operate a state-funded law school of equal quality for black citizens, or force the University of Maryland to admit Murray and other black students.

In June 1935, Baltimore city judge Eugene O'Dunne heard arguments from both sides. The university argued that the state provided scholarships for black students to attend schools outside of Maryland, which would have provided them an equal education. Additionally, the university contended that not admitting black students was "a long-standing public policy," not an instance of racial prejudice. Finally, the school's dean pointed out that there was no significant demand for law schools among black students. Each of these arguments proved relatively weak when placed against the case Marshall formulated with the NAACP.

First, Marshall indicated that Murray had been consistently placed on the dean's list at his undergraduate institution. Based solely on his academic performance, Maryland's law school should have admitted Murray easily. Second, sending black students to schools in other states on scholarship was a violation of the state's responsibility to the Fourteenth Amendment. Third, Marshall argued that the state had lived up to its obligation to provide separate facilities, as outlined in *Plessy*, but it had not lived up to the equality of those institutions. In essence, the 1896 case had required institutions be "separate but equal," not separate *or* equal. Finally, Marshall appealed to the spirit of equality as outlined in the Constitution. "What's at stake," Marshall stated in his

A seated Donald Gaines Murray (*center*) listens to Thurgood Marshall as they prepare to argue his case.

closing argument, "is more than just the rights of my client. It's the moral commitment stated in our country's creed."

Judge O'Dunne sided with Marshall. The University of Maryland tried to appeal O'Dunne's decision, but in October, the Maryland Court of Appeals issued an opinion that solidified the ruling in favor of Murray. In the **judicial opinion**, Justice Carroll Bond wrote:

> The case, as we find it, then, is that the State has undertaken the function of education of the law, but has omitted students of one race from the only adequate provision made for it, and omitted them solely because of their color. If those students are to be offered equal treatment in the performance of the function, they must, at present, be admitted to the one school provided.

No Equal Opportunity

Forward Thinking

Charles Hamilton Houston proved one of the most significant, lasting influences on Thurgood Marshall's career. Born in 1895, Houston served in the United States Army during World War I. Then Houston earned his law degree and a doctorate in juridical science from Harvard University. Houston became the head of Howard University's law school in 1929, where he transformed the school into a workshop for young black lawyers "so that Negroes could gain equality by fighting segregation in the courts." In 1935, Houston became a key attorney for the NAACP, through which he, Thurgood Marshall, and other activist attorneys would challenge school segregation at the state and national levels.

In 1978, Marshall spoke to an event honoring Houston at Amherst College. Marshall opened his address saying, "I am not one to believe in looking back. I believe in looking forward. And we have to look at Charlie Houston because he looked forward." To Marshall, and many other civil rights activists, Charles Hamilton Houston served as a key inspiration to challenge the legality of segregation in the United States.

In its ruling, the Maryland Court of Appeals supported Houston and Marshall's strategy. The university admitted Murray, and the precedent existed to challenge other states that did not provide "adequate" institutions for students of all races. Houston, Marshall, and the NAACP began a twenty-year legal crusade against school segregation founded on the judicial standard set in *Murray v. Pearson*.

In 1938, Houston argued *Missouri ex rel. Gaines v. Canada* before the Supreme Court. The court ruled that any state maintaining one public law school, like Maryland, "may not limit admission by race." Later, Marshall attacked the practice of white-only primary elections that many Southern states used. In white-only primaries, some states did not allow black voters to cast a ballot in the primary election for government officials. Black voters in white-only primary states were often forced in the general election to choose between two candidates who were both segregationists. The Supreme Court declared this practice unconstitutional after hearing Marshall's argument in *Smith v. Allwright* in 1944. Two years later, in *Morgan v. Virginia*, Marshall swayed the Supreme Court to end the practice of segregation in bus transportation between states. This victory, combined with Marshall's later argument in the 1960 case *Boynton v. Virginia*, eventually prompted the famous "Freedom Ride" movement of the civil rights era. Freedom Riders left Washington, DC, and toured the South, attempting to integrate bus stations and the restrooms and lunch counters in those stations.

In 1947, Marshall convinced the Supreme Court that juries selected from whites only could not convict African Americans. Marshall won twenty-nine of thirty-two cases in front of the Supreme Court. The cases argued against segregation in various institutions, though they all stemmed from Marshall's central issue: desegregation of public schools.

Early in their partnership, Charles Houston and Marshall concentrated on the admissions policies of graduate schools. Because there were fewer students, examples of inequality were easier to pinpoint. However, cases like *Murray* and *Gaines* provided the NAACP with a legal argument that could potentially extend to all schools. They received their opportunity when two families in Clarendon County, South Carolina, petitioned for "equalization" of the public schools provided by the county. When Marshall heard about the case, he convinced one of the families, headed by Harry and Liza

Briggs, to include in their lawsuit "a claim that segregation in public education was in and of itself unconstitutional."

Marshall lost his case in the state court, but he and the NAACP appealed it to the Supreme Court. The court sent the case back to the South Carolina district courts so that it could determine whether or not the state was attempting to provide equal schooling for black and white students. However, Marshall and the NAACP chose to consolidate the Briggs case with four other cases that had been brought against the segregation of schools: *Davis et al. v. County School Board of Prince Edward County, Virginia*; *Gebhard v. Belton*; *Bolling v. Sharpe*; and finally, the case's namesake, ***Brown v. Board of Education of Topeka***. Now, with five separate cases of segregation brought into one lawsuit, Thurgood Marshall and the NAACP would argue for an end to the segregation of public schools in the United States.

Marshall composed an argument that included the testimony and research of Dr. Kenneth Clark, a black sociologist. Clark demonstrated that segregation had negative effects on the mental development of black children. In his "doll tests," Clark showed that children associated black dolls with worse characteristics than white dolls after being exposed to early education in segregated schools. Clark stated, "What was surprising was the degree to which children suffered … I don't think we had quite realized the extent of the cruelty of racism and how hard it hit."

John W. Davis, the defense attorney, defended segregation and the "Southern way of life." He argued that segregation was good for the development of both races. Davis believed that there were differences between the races that made separate education necessary. In a letter to a colleague before arguing the *Brown* case, Davis said, "Is it not conceivable that in addition to the anatomical differences [between black and white students] there are also differences in the intellectual processes, in tastes and in aptitudes?" Marshall and his team of lawyers from the NAACP sought to prove Davis wrong.

The student plaintiffs in the *Brown v. Board of Education of Topeka* case in 1954 were (*front row from left*) Vicki and Donald Henderson, Linda Brown, James Emanuel, Nancy Todd, and Katherine Carper. Behind them are parents Zelma Henderson, Oliver Brown, Sadie Emanuel, Linda Todd, and Lena Carper.

Throughout the case, Marshall argued against the basis for segregation. He suggested there were no meaningful distinctions between races that would require school segregation. Therefore, the Fourteenth Amendment must provide equal treatment under any legal institution, including publicly provided schools. He maintained that segregation based on race was also illogical. Marshall stated, "[The segregationists] would have to show—and we have shown to the contrary—they would have to show one, that there are differences in race; and two, that differences in race have a recognizable relationship to the subject matter being legislated, namely, public education." The defense would have to prove that black and white children were substantially different and that those differences had an effect on education.

The attorneys for the defense certainly tried. Davis's closing arguments threatened that desegregation would destroy the "present order" of American society. Davis contended Southern states like South Carolina intended to create equal facilities for students of all races. A constitutional requirement to do so would spur radical opposition, and it would slow progress toward equal education.

The statements in Marshall's closing argument were a departure from tradition and precedent. Marshall argued, "These children in these cases are guaranteed by the states some twelve years of education in varying degrees." The states, Marshall contended, could take their time in providing equal institutions, so long as they proved to be attempting to "work it out." Davis had argued the court must be restrained or limited in its action. It could not just simply tell the states what to do. Marshall argued, "The argument of judicial restraint has no application in this case. There is a relationship between federal and state, but there is no ... relationship as to the Fourteenth Amendment. The duty of following the Fourteenth Amendment is placed upon the states. The duty of enforcing the Fourteenth Amendment is placed upon this Court." Marshall argued segregation was the product of Black Codes, laws that restricted the freedom of former slaves as early as the Reconstruction period. "Nobody has done anything," Marshall contended, "to distinguish this statute [segregation] from the Black Codes." If segregating public schools was an extension of the Black Codes, it was an attempt by the states to make sure "that the people who were formerly in slavery, regardless of anything else, shall be kept as near that stage as is possible." In summation, Marshall had proven that segregation was an attempt to destroy the equality of freed slaves and their descendants. Congress passed the Thirteenth, Fourteenth, and Fifteenth Amendments after the Civil War to prevent this treatment. Therefore, segregation is fundamentally unconstitutional.

Marshall's impressive connection won the court's opinion. In a historic 9–0 decision, Chief Justice Earl Warren wrote the only opinion of the court that banned segregation in public schools. Warren wrote:

Thurgood Marshall and *Brown v. Board of Education of Topeka*

Today, education is perhaps the most important function of state and local governments … It is a principal instrument in awakening the child to cultural values, in preparing him for later professional training, and in helping him to adjust normally to his environment … Such an opportunity, where the state has undertaken to provide it, is a right which must be made available to all on equal terms.

The legal team of George Hayes, Thurgood Marshall, and James Nabrit pose on the steps of the Supreme Court building in Washington, DC, after winning the landmark *Brown v. Board of Education of Topeka* case.

guage in *Plessy* v. *Ferguson* contrary to this finding is rejected.

We conclude that in the field of public education the doctrine of "separate but equal" has no place. Separate educational facilities are inherently unequal. Therefore, we hold that the plaintiffs and others similarly situated for whom the actions have been brought are, by reason of the segregation complained of, deprived of the equal protection of the laws guaranteed by the Fourteenth Amendment. This disposition makes unnecessary any discussion whether such segregation also violates the Due Process Clause of the Fourteenth Amendment.[12]

Because these are class actions, because of the wide applicability of this decision, and because of the great variety of local conditions, the formulation of decrees in these cases presents problems of considerable complexity. On reargument, the consideration of appropriate relief was necessarily subordinated to the primary question—the constitutionality of segregation in public education. We have now announced that such segregation is a denial of the equal protection of the laws. In order that we may have the full assistance of the parties in formulating decrees, the cases will be restored to the docket, and the parties are requested to present further argument on Questions 4 and 5 previously propounded by the Court for the reargument this Term.[13]   The Attorney General

---

[12] See *Bolling* v. *Sharpe, infra,* concerning the Due Process Clause of the Fifth Amendment.

[13] "4. Assuming it is decided that segregation in public schools violates the Fourteenth Amendment

"(*a*) would a decree necessarily follow providing that, within the limits set by normal geographic school districting, Negro children should forthwith be admitted to schools of their choice, or

"(*b*) may this Court, in the exercise of its equity powers, permit an effective gradual adjustment to be brought about from existing segregated systems to a system not based on color distinctions?

"5. On the assumption on which questions 4 (*a*) and (*b*) are

In the paragraph marked from his opinion in the *Brown v. Board of Education* case, Chief Justice Earl Warren states the doctrine of "separate but equal" has no place in public education and that "separate educational facilities are inherently unequal."

Thurgood Marshall and *Brown v. Board of Education of Topeka*

People line up at the Supreme Court to hear oral arguments in the *Brown v. Board of Education of Topeka* case.

By inserting the necessity for "equal terms" of education, Warren was affirming Marshall and Houston's arguments. If not provided equally, education could be a means of oppression. Warren condemned the idea of separate but equal emphatically in his opinion.

In one action, the Supreme Court declared any segregation of public schools based on race in violation of the Constitution. The long-sought dream of Marshall, his mentor Houston, the NAACP, and millions of African Americans was achieved.

Significantly, the ruling did not translate into immediate justice for all black Americans. Three years after the ruling, Arkansas governor Orval Faubus refused to admit nine African-American students to Central High School in the

US Marshalls escort James Meredith through a crowd of protestors after registering for classes at the University of Mississippi. Meredith was the first African-American to do so.

state's capital of Little Rock. Marshall himself sued Faubus, which prompted President Dwight D. Eisenhower, a cautious supporter of civil rights, to issue Executive Order 10730. In the order, Eisenhower used his authority as commander in chief to force Arkansas to comply with national law. In his famous address to the nation, Eisenhower stated, "I have today issued an Executive Order directing the use of troops under Federal authority to aid in the execution of Federal law at Little Rock, Arkansas." Eisenhower condemned the actions of "mobs" that attempted to ignore federal law. He argued, "The very basis of our individual rights and freedoms rests upon the certainty that the President ... will support and insure the carrying out of the decisions of the Federal Courts, even, when necessary with all the means at the President's command." Eisenhower used force to mandate compliance with the *Brown* decision. The ruling,

Thurgood Marshall and *Brown v. Board of Education of Topeka*

Eisenhower said, would provide for "one nation, indivisible, with liberty and justice for all."

Opposition to *Brown v. Board* continued, however. In 1962, James Meredith, a black veteran, enrolled in the University of Mississippi and prompted a massive community riot. In 1962, George C. Wallace, was elected governor of Alabama. In his inaugural address on January 14, 1963, Wallace declared:

> Let us send this message back to Washington, via the representatives who are here with us today. From this day, we are standing up, and the heel of tyranny does not fit the neck of an upright man. Let us rise to the call of freedom-loving blood that is in us, and send our answer to the tyranny that clanks its chains upon the South. In the name of the greatest people that have ever trod this earth, I draw a line in the dust and toss the gauntlet before the feet of tyranny, and I say, segregation now, segregation tomorrow and segregation forever.

In June of 1963, Wallace blocked the entrance door to the state's university as two black students attempted to enter. In the same period, figures like Martin Luther King Jr., Malcolm X, John Lewis, and Stokely Carmichael would march for civil rights legislation in the nation's most iconic struggle for the promise of equality. The court's ruling in *Brown v. Board of Education* mobilized these forces. However, for Thurgood Marshall, this struggle was only just beginning.

Seven members of the "Little Rock Nine"—students who wanted to enter Little Rock, Arkansas' Central High School after the ruling in *Brown*, join Thurgood Marshall on the steps of the Supreme Court, where Marshall would appeal the governor of Arkansas's decision to refuse their entrance to the school.

Position of Influence

T he *Brown v. Board* ruling affected America and Thurgood Marshall. After the ruling, Marshall and the NAACP began working on a plan for integration. Due to political realities, President Eisenhower and Chief Justice Earl Warren both agreed to demand states only integrate "with all deliberate speed." This contradicted the 1956 deadline for nationwide integration that Marshall had proposed. At the same time, Marshall criticized the growth of black militancy. Tragedies like the murder of fourteen-year-old Emmett Till marked this aggressive turn in the civil rights movement. When Martin Luther King Jr. led the Montgomery bus boycotts, Marshall was supportive, but cautious. King often operated without the consent or involvement of the NAACP because the organization had different plans for ending inequality. Publicly, however, Marshall remained a strong supporter of King and his nonviolent movement.

Marshall also got involved in the situation in Little Rock, Arkansas, at the request of the NAACP. In 1957, before flying to Little Rock to file suit against the state, Marshall gave an interview to *Newsweek*, in which he specified his stance on the process of integration. Many politicians and public figures feared an approach to integration of schools that was not "gradualist," one that would allow for adjustment to the new institutions. When asked about his reaction to gradualism by the magazine, Marshall replied,

> I'm the original gradualist. But let's make sure what we're talking about. If by gradualism you mean a policy of doing nothing, letting things drift and hoping for the best, I'm dead set against it … We intend to work this out in an orderly fashion … We are making progress … In general we are completely optimistic.

Marshall aimed to finish what he had started. The integration mandated by the *Brown* decision needed to be enforced if it was to succeed.

Marshall soon realized the limitations of his power as counsel for the NAACP. Though he argued several cases under the precedent set by *Brown*, Marshall became anxious to continue promoting civil rights throughout the nation. In 1960, Georgia police arrested various activists, including the nationally recognized Martin Luther King Jr., following a sit-in movement for civil rights. The Democratic Party's candidate for president, John F. Kennedy, instructed Robert Kennedy, his younger brother and campaign manager, to call for King's release. Though Republican candidate Richard Nixon ran a close campaign, Kennedy's advocacy for King's release won him 68 percent of the African-American vote and the presidency.

President Kennedy supported civil rights reform and legislation. Marshall was skeptical of Kennedy's dedication

Thurgood Marshall and *Brown v. Board of Education of Topeka*

after he did not introduce any civil rights bills in his first one hundred days in office. In response to criticism and in an effort to advance civil rights activism, Robert Kennedy, the new attorney general of the United States, wanted to place Marshall on a federal district court. Marshall, however, wanted placement on the Federal Court of Appeals, just one step below the Supreme Court. Kennedy only offered him a district court spot, and Marshall held fast. When Kennedy told him, "It's that or nothing," Marshall bluntly stated, "Well, I've been dealing with nothing all my life, there's nothing new on that."

Soon, the Kennedy administration gave in. They appointed Marshall to the Federal Court of Appeals. After a long battle over his confirmation, Marshall took his position on the court in 1961. He rebuffed every challenge by segregationist senators. One senator questioned Marshall's statement that God was on the side of the NAACP. Anyone against the institution was, by implication, working for Satan. Marshall replied that many of the organization's opponents were members of the Ku Klux Klan, and "anyone who takes a man out and lynches him, I believe is working with the devil."

As a federal judge, Marshall heard many important cases regarding labor laws, financial reform, and other issues. He traveled to Africa to promote civil rights and economic development. When he returned, he dissented from several appeals court decisions, including one where he stated, "Desegregation obviously has not proceeded as fast as we would have liked." As he drew more attention, Marshall became a candidate for a more influential position.

In November 1963, Lee Harvey Oswald assassinated President John F. Kennedy in Dallas, Texas. Vice President Lyndon Johnson, a former senator from Texas, succeeded Kennedy. Within two years of assuming the office, Johnson had overseen several efforts toward civil rights reform. The Civil Rights Act of 1964 banned segregation, and the Voting Rights Act of 1965 made efforts to limit access to voting

Face of Change

Not all politicians accepted integration as a viable option for their states. In particular, many Southern governors attempted to resist integration. They argued aggressively that segregation was, in fact, a policy that was best for both black and white students.

Arkansas governor Orval Faubus contended in his 1958 "Speech on School Integration":

> The Supreme Court shut its eyes to all the facts, and in essence said—integration at any price, even if it means the destruction of our school system, our educational processes, and the risk of disorder and violence that could result in the loss of life—perhaps yours.

On his television show, Arkansas governor Orval Faubus displays a newspaper headline stating "Anger and Threats Mar School Opening" to bolster his support of segregation.

Thurgood Marshall and *Brown v. Board of Education of Topeka*

Dr. Kenneth B. Clark, an African-American behavioral scientist, documented the negative effects on black students of school segregation.

In the "Dolls Test," Dr. Kenneth Clark and his wife, Mamie, showed segregation's damaging effects and proved segregated educational environments fostered racism in children's minds. In an interview with PBS for a documentary on the civil rights movement, Clark recalled:

> The Dolls Test was an attempt on the part of my wife and me to study the development of the sense of self-esteem in children. We worked with Negro children … to see the extent to which their color, their sense of their own race and status, influenced their judgment about themselves, self-esteem. We did it to communicate to our colleagues in psychology the influence of race and color and status on the self-esteem of children.

President Lyndon Johnson congratulates Thurgood Marshall after he is sworn in as the nation's first African-American solicitor general in 1965.

rights on the basis of race illegal. Johnson followed these moves by nominating Thurgood Marshall to the position of **solicitor general**, the number two attorney for the United States government, just under the attorney general. In one of his first cases as solicitor general, Marshall brought federal charges against the murderers of three civil rights activists in Mississippi. Marshall argued the killers acted to frighten black

Thurgood Marshall and *Brown v. Board of Education of Topeka*

Mississippians from exercising their rights. Unanimously, the court agreed, stating the men "were part of a plan and conspiracy" to infringe on African Americans' rights. In another case, Marshall successfully tried the state of Virginia for violating the Twenty-Fourth Amendment, which had banned poll taxes, or fees charged to black voters at the polling center.

In 1967, two years after Marshall's nomination as solicitor general, Lyndon Johnson made a historic decision. On June 13, Johnson announced he was nominating Solicitor General Thurgood Marshall to fill a vacancy on the Supreme Court of the United States. "I believe he has already earned his place in history, but I think it will be greatly enhanced by his service on the Court ... He is best qualified by training and by very valuable service to the country. I believe it is the right thing to do, the right time to do it, the right man and the right place," Johnson said. After a three-month battle over his confirmation in the senate, Marshall took the oath of office as the first African-American associate justice of the Supreme Court of the United States on September 1, 1967.

Marshall's appointment proved the lasting impact of the *Brown v. Board* decision. As an attorney, Marshall had advocated that the Fourteenth Amendment justified equality under law. Now, serving on the highest court in the nation, Marshall had the opportunity to apply that principle across many legal issues. Though committed to education, Marshall also dedicated himself to advancing equality in many other areas. In his first opinion for the court, Marshall ruled in *Mempa v. Rhay* that a lawyer must be provided to any person brought before a court, regardless of his or her past criminal status. The court ruled unanimously on Marshall's side, and he provided the court's opinion "with brevity, clarity, and force," in the opinion of Associate Justice Hugo Black. Quickly, Marshall became a respected member of the court.

In 1968, Martin Luther King Jr. was shot and killed in Memphis, Tennessee. This moment profoundly shaped

Thurgood Marshall is joined in 1967 by his sons, Thurgood Jr. and John, and his wife, Cecilia Suyat, before taking his seat as a Supreme Court associate justice for the first time.

the nation's efforts toward equality. Movements like "Black Power" and other militant organizations grew in number and influence. Marshall, consistently suspicious of any mass demonstration, particularly violent ones, struggled with these changes. In an address at Dillard University, Marshall condemned the actions of violent protestors. "It takes no courage to get in the back of a crowd and throw a rock,"

Thurgood Marshall and *Brown v. Board of Education of Topeka*

Marshall said. "Rather, it takes courage to stand up on your own two feet and look anyone straight in the eye and say, 'I will not be beaten.'"

As an associate justice, Marshall could most impact civil rights through Supreme Court rulings. In various cases, Marshall advocated for the rights of "organized labor, racial minorities, the advancement of women, the broadening of rights to freedom of expression, and the narrowing of police authority," according to Harvard professor Randall L. Kennedy. In *Police Department of the City of Chicago v. Mosley*, the Supreme Court ruled that a government body could not limit the content of protests. Therefore, the police department could not allow some protests and not others. In his majority opinion, Marshall wrote, "Above all else, the First Amendment means that government has no power to restrict expression because of its message, its ideas, its subject matter, or its content … Our people are guaranteed the right to express any thought, free from government censorship." Marshall became a central advocate for equality under the law.

In the landmark case ***Regents of the University of California v. Bakke***, the Supreme Court tackled a complex issue of race and education. The University of California used race as a factor in determining an applicant's admission. The goal of the program was to make sure that minority candidates who may have been previously disadvantaged due to unequal educational resources would have a competitive opportunity for admission. Allan Bakke had applied to the university's medical school at Davis and been rejected. Bakke, a white man, argued that he had been denied admission based on his race, and that such a rejection violated the Fourteenth Amendment. In a complicated ruling, the court admitted Bakke to the institution, arguing that he was a prime candidate for admission. The court also ruled that the university's policy of factoring race into admissions decisions, a policy known as "**affirmative action**,"

Allan Bakke received his degree in medicine from the University of California at Davis in 1982. When denied entry to medical school, he successfully sued claiming racial discrimination in the institution's use of affirmative action programs.

was constitutional and permissible. In a concurring opinion, Justice Marshall disagreed with the court's decision to admit Bakke, but agreed with the court's decision to allow race to be a factor in admissions decisions. Marshall wrote:

> I fear that we have come full circle. After the Civil War, our Government started several "affirmative action" programs. This Court, in the *Civil Rights Cases* and *Plessy v. Ferguson*, destroyed the movement toward complete equality. For almost a century, no action was

Thurgood Marshall and *Brown v. Board of Education of Topeka*

taken, and this nonaction was with the tacit approval of the courts. Then we had *Brown v. Board of Education* and the Civil Rights Acts of Congress, followed by numerous affirmative action programs. Now, we have this court again stepping in, this time to stop affirmative action programs of the type used by the University of California.

In Marshall's mind, admitting Bakke undermined affirmative action programs. Marshall's opinion accurately predicted the growth of criticism for affirmative action. These programs were not, in the justice's opinion, unfair preference toward minorities. Instead, they served as attempts to provide equal opportunity, especially for those disadvantaged by corrupt legal decisions for centuries. Marshall stated, "The racism of our society has been so pervasive that none … has managed to escape its impact." In *Bakke*, Marshall feared that the court had set a precedent for undoing the work accomplished through *Brown v. Board* and the civil rights movement. As the only justice on the court who could personally attest to the reality of racism, Marshall became a key advocate for equality, justice, and freedom as a leader of the nation's highest judicial institution.

Impact from the Bench

As an associate justice, Marshall made an impact on the nation's consideration of civil rights and issues of equality. In 1974, the Supreme Court heard arguments in a case that dealt with federal court rulings that forced a plan for desegregation on schools outside of Detroit, Michigan. The state maintained it did not have to follow the federal ruling, as it was not out of compliance with *Brown v. Board*. In a 5–4 decision, the court held that the state would be allowed to conduct its own integration of schools. In dissent, or disagreement, Marshall joined three other justices vigorously against the court's decision.

> Desegregation is not and was never expected to be an easy task … But just as the inconvenience of some cannot be allowed to stand in the way of the rights of others, so public opposition, no

A Central High School student verbally harasses Elizabeth Eckford, one of the "Little Rock Nine," as she heads for the entrance of the newly integrated school.

matter how strident, cannot be permitted to divert this Court from the enforcement of the constitutional principles at issue in the case … It may seem to be the easier course to allow our great metropolitan areas to be divided up each into two cities—one white, the other black— but it is a course, I predict, our people will ultimately regret.

Marshall feared that allowing cities to avoid desegregation on the basis of their own integration laws would create a racial divide in the nation's cities.

In 1989, Marshall again found himself dissenting against his fellow justices in *City of Richmond v. J.A. Croson Company*. The city of Richmond, Virginia, had required 30 percent of the city's construction projects to go to businesses owned by minorities. This was an attempt to enforce equal opportunity in the economy. Writing for the majority, Justice Sandra Day O'Connor argued that "generalized assertions" of discriminations in history did not justify this program. Marshall contended, "Nothing in the Constitution can be construed to prevent Richmond, Virginia, from allocating a portion of its contracting dollars for businesses owned or controlled by members of minority groups."

Marshall found it "a welcome symbol of racial progress" that "the former capital of the Confederacy" would seek to provide opportunities for minority citizens. Marshall hated that the court had now used the Fourteenth Amendment, which was established to erase the wrongs of post–Civil War inequality, to strike down an effort by a community to make its economy and society more diverse and tolerant. He contended, "A profound difference separates governmental actions that themselves are racist, and governmental actions that seek to remedy the effects of prior racism." Richmond was attempting to undo the damage of segregation. Disappointed in the court's decision, Marshall ended his opinion, "The battle against pernicious racial discrimination or its effects is nowhere near won."

Throughout his professional career, Marshall wrote at length of the importance of protecting equal rights and the legacy of *Brown v. Board*. In the *Washington University Law Quarterly* of 1967, then-Solicitor General Marshall wrote of the importance of legal enforcement and advancement of the *Brown* decision. He pointed out that for decades after the Civil War, the nation had misused the Fourteenth Amendment. It "became not an effective shield for human rights, as it had been intended," Marshall observed, "but

Thurgood Marshall and *Brown v. Board of Education of Topeka*

James Meredith sits in a mathematics class at the University of Mississippi in 1962.

rather a mechanism by which corporations took on human traits and enjoyed the protections of what became known as substantive due process." Economic gain, Marshall claimed, was more important to the nation after the Civil War than protections of black Americans' civil rights. Marshall then traced the historic development of anti-segregation law, arguing that *Brown v. Board* set in motion a series of events emancipating African Americans from discrimination. In the article, Marshall wrote, "Law is often a response to social change; but as I think *Brown v. Board of Education* demonstrates, it also can change social patterns … Law can change things for the better; moreover, it can change the hearts of men, for law has an educational function also."

Toward the end of his legal career, Marshall feared that society was regressing in its advocacy for civil rights. In an address to the Second Circuit Judicial Conference in 1989, Marshall discussed the fact that the growth of conservative ideas on the court had led to a decline in the court's advocacy for individual liberties and the rights of minorities. "History teaches," said Marshall, "that when the Supreme Court has been willing to shortchange the equality rights of minority groups, other basic personal civil liberties … are also threatened." Above all, Marshall feared "complacency." For Marshall, the injustices of the past were all too real to ignore. The court had to stand up for individual and civil rights, at whatever cost.

In 1987, Marshall wrote an article for a symposium on the Bill of Rights during the nation's bicentennial celebrations of the Constitution. In what was nationally "dedicated to the memory of the Founders and the document they drafted in Philadelphia," the event proved to bring out, in Marshall's view, "patriotic feelings … [and] proud proclamations of the wisdom, foresight, and sense of justice shared by the Founders." However, Marshall was not as willing to celebrate the Constitution as other legal experts were in 1987. Instead, Marshall wrote, "I cannot accept this invitation, for I do not believe that the meaning of the Constitution was forever 'fixed' at the Philadelphia Convention."

Marshall's view seems logical. The Constitution signed in 1787 excluded women, African Americans, and men without property from voting, and it did not condemn or prohibit slavery. Marshall looked at the Constitution itself, showing it took "several amendments, a civil war, and momentous social transformation to attain the system of constitutional government, and its respect for the individual freedoms and

Exporting Equality

In 1960, Kenyan politicians who wanted to achieve further independence from Great Britain invited Thurgood Marshall to assist in their formation of legal institutions. At a conference with British and Kenyan leaders, Marshall helped craft a Kenyan Bill of Rights. Marshall combined principles of American law with the United Nations' Universal Declaration of Human Rights to form the basis of the document. In 1963, Kenya declared its independence from Britain.

Even after his appointment to the Supreme Court, Marshall would continue to advocate for global justice. In 1977, Marshall addressed the Eighth Conference on the Law of the World, calling for collective action toward a more just world. Marshall stated, "World peace through law is a magnificent goal … When I think back on my own life, the changes I have seen, a few perhaps that I helped to cause, there is reason to hope. But there is so much more to be done if justice and peace are to become a way of life for every person on Earth."

human rights, we hold as fundamental today." For Marshall, the Constitution was an "evolving" idea that must be changed from time to time.

Marshall became a firm defender of this view toward a living Constitution, one that could change and adapt to the times. Indeed, Marshall's own career proved that the vision of the Founding Fathers was incomplete, one that did not afford all men and women freedom and equality. Therefore, Marshall advocated that Americans should not fear criticizing their government and its institutions. In *Brown v. Board*, Marshall

President Ronald Reagan (*first row, third from right*) poses with the justices of the Supreme Court in 1982, with Thurgood Marshall seated on the far left.

argued against the "Southern tradition" of segregation. His later career saw the same opposition to traditional interpretations of government. Marshall told Americans, in his "Reflections on the Bicentennial of the United States Constitution":

> If we seek, instead, a sensitive understanding of the Constitution's inherent defects, and its promising evolution through 200 years of history, the celebration of the "Miracle at Philadelphia" will, in my view, be a far more meaningful and humbling experience. We will see that the true miracle was not the birth of the Constitution, but its life, a life nurtured through two turbulent centuries of our own making, and a life embodying much good fortune that was not.

Thurgood Marshall and *Brown v. Board of Education of Topeka*

Marshall's career became an example of the idea of the Constitution as this living document. Marshall wanted to help improve the document and its ideas, principles, and mission. Truly, he wanted "to establish a more perfect union."

In 1978, Marshall gave the commencement address at the University of Virginia. Founded by Thomas Jefferson, the institution became an important academic center of learning about law, politics, and history. Jefferson, author of the Declaration of Independence, was not exempt from the culture of his society. He owned slaves, and in fact, slave labor helped establish the physical foundation of the university some two hundred years before Marshall's address. It was quite historic that an African-American associate justice on the Supreme Court would be the keynote speaker at the school's graduation ceremony. In his address, Marshall praised the foresight and wisdom of Mr. Jefferson, particularly his explanation of the core values of American society in the declaration of 1776. Marshall commented, "For me, [America's] cardinal principle is that all persons stand in a position of equality before the law." Here, twenty years after the ruling in *Brown v. Board*, Marshall was still emphasizing the importance of the Fourteenth Amendment as confirming this spirit of American government.

Marshall's address cut to the very core of his pursuits as a civil rights leader. He said to the graduates:

> There are still far too many persons in this country who cannot participate as equals in the process of government—persons too poor, too ignorant, persons discriminated against by other people for no good reason. But our ideal, the ideal of our Constitution, is to eliminate these barriers …

Thus, for Marshall, the United States had never been a perfectly formed nation. It was a nation that must change and progress. "This is a great country," Marshall explained in the address. "But fortunately for you it is not perfect. There is much to be done to bring about complete equality … This is your democracy. Make it, protect it, pass it on."

Thurgood Marshall's career in law spanned over sixty years, and it profoundly changed American society. Even after it was over, he continued to pursue equality. His work for the NAACP in cases like *Murray v. Pearson* and *Brown v. Board* established legal precedent to end segregation. His work as federal judge and solicitor general set an example for government officials of the future to help the oppressed. His career as an associate justice on the United States Supreme Court proved an example of the greatness a society shows when it treats its citizens equally. He fought, throughout his life, for those who were victims of injustice. Most impressively, Marshall used the principles of justice and law to right those wrongs, to hold governments accountable to their citizens, and to help the United States live up to its promise of equality to all Americans.

In January 1863, President Abraham Lincoln famously issued the Emancipation Proclamation, a formative moment in the nation's history. With this statement, Lincoln transformed the Civil War into a war to end slavery wherever it existed. Lincoln also positioned the United States as a nation that would, at whatever cost, fight for the freedom of all its citizens. Three weeks after he issued the proclamation, President Lincoln wrote to Major General Joseph Hooker of the Union army. Empowered by the Union's reformed purpose—to bring an end to slavery—Lincoln implored Hooker: "Beware of rashness, but with energy, and sleepless vigilance, go forward, and give us victories." As Thurgood Marshall resigned his position as associate justice on June 27, 1991, the words of the

A poster, later colorized, of President Abraham Lincoln's Emancipation Proclamation publicized the first federal declaration used to end slavery.

Great Emancipator seem to be a fitting summary of Marshall's storied career. He was a man who, with "sleepless vigilance," pursued the same victory Lincoln sought: freedom, justice, and liberty for all Americans.

Chronology

Dates in green pertain to events discussed in this volume.

1863 The Emancipation Proclamation is issued by President Abraham Lincoln.

1865 The Thirteenth Amendment, abolishing slavery, is passed in the US House of Representatives. The amendment was passed by the Senate in 1864.

1868 The Fourteenth Amendment, guaranteeing equal rights under the law, is passed.

1870 The Fifteenth Amendment, prohibiting governments from denying male citizens the right to vote based on their race, is passed.

1883 The Supreme Court strikes down the Civil Rights Act of 1875, which guaranteed equal rights to all African Americans in transportation, restaurants or inns, theaters, and on juries.

1896 *Plessy v. Ferguson*, establishing the precedent of "separate but equal," is handed down by the Supreme Court of the United States.

1908 Thurgood Marshall is born in Baltimore, Maryland.

1909 The National Association for the Advancement of Colored People (NAACP) is established.

1935 Thurgood Marshall and

Charles Hamilton Houston successfully sue the University of Maryland, arguing for Donald Murray's admission to the institution's law school in *Murray v. Pearson*. The two argue that as the state does not provide a public law school for African Americans, it does not provide adequate "separate but equal" institutions.

1941 President Franklin D. Roosevelt bans discrimination against minorities in the granting of defense contracts.

1944 Thurgood Marshall successfully argues the Supreme Court case *Smith v. Allwright*, which eliminates the South's use of all-white primary elections.

1954 Thurgood Marshall and the NAACP win the case of *Brown v. Board of Education of Topeka*, which overturns *Plessy v. Ferguson* and the "separate but equal" doctrine of segregation in the United States.

1955 Rosa Parks refuses to give up her seat to a white person on a bus in Montgomery, Alabama. Her arrest sparks a bus boycott.

1957 Federal troops are called in to protect nine African-American students in Little Rock, Arkansas, who

Thurgood Marshall and *Brown v. Board of Education of Topeka*

are trying to attend all-white Central High School.

1960 President John F. Kennedy issues an executive order prohibiting discrimination in federal hiring on the basis of race, religion, or national origin.

1961 Congress on Racial Equality organizes Freedom Rides throughout the South, and the riders suffer beatings from mobs in many cities.

1961 Thurgood Marshall wins the circuit court case *Garner v. Louisiana* in defense of demonstrators arguing for civil rights. After this defense, President John F. Kennedy nominates Marshall to the Second Federal Court of Appeals.

1963 The March on Washington attracts a quarter of a million people, who listen to Martin Luther King Jr.'s "I Have a Dream" speech.

1964 President Lyndon B. Johnson signs the Civil Rights Act of 1964. It prohibits discrimination of all kinds.

1965 When an effort to register black voters is met with resistance in the South, Martin Luther King Jr. and the Southern Christian Leadership Conference organize a march for voting rights in Alabama from Selma to Montgomery. Later in the year, Congress passes the Voting Rights Act, which guarantees to all African Americans the right to vote.

1967 Thurgood Marshall becomes the first African-American Supreme Court justice. He is nominated by President Lyndon B. Johnson.

1967 The Supreme Court rules that laws prohibiting interracial marriage are unconstitutional. Sixteen states are required to change their laws.

1968 Martin Luther King Jr. is assassinated in Memphis, Tennessee, while supporting a sanitation workers strike.

1991 Thurgood Marshall retires from the court after a twenty-four-year tenure. Marshall's decisions helped define modern civil rights and steered the contemporary movement for black equality.

1993 Thurgood Marshall dies at the age of eighty-four.

2003 The Supreme Court upholds a policy at the University of Michigan Law School, ruling that race can be used as a consideration in admitting students.

Glossary

affirmative action The practice of factoring race into admission decisions of colleges and universities. The policy is an attempt to "level the playing field" for students of all races and allow minorities more access to college admission.

Brown v. Board of Education of Topeka In 1954, the Supreme Court under Chief Justice Earl Warren ruled that segregation of public schools violated the Fourteenth Amendment to the United States Constitution, which mandated "equal protection of the laws" to all citizens, black or white. This decision overturned the doctrine established in *Plessy v. Ferguson*, and it made segregation illegal.

equality The state of being the same in value, rights, opportunities, and status.

integration The process through which the United States government eliminated segregation (separation of the races), by allowing persons of all races access to the same public resources, including schools.

judicial opinion A written explanation of a court's ruling in a particular case. These opinions often contain important descriptions of legal principles that factor into a court's decisions. Opinions can side with the majority in the court's ruling or dissent from it with the minority against the court's ruling.

legal counsel A lawyer who represents a group or person in a court of law.

lynching A mob-run, localized system of carrying out punishment for perceived crimes that often included kidnapping, torturing, and executing a victim. Lynching became a tactic used to suppress, intimidate, and eliminate African Americans.

National Association for the Advancement of Colored People An organization founded by W. E. B. Du Bois in 1909 to advance the cause of black equality. The NAACP is the oldest civil rights institution in the nation.

Plessy v. Ferguson Decided in 1896, this Supreme Court case ruled against a man with African-American heritage named Homer Plessy, who sued Louisiana for being forced off a train for refusing to move to a separate railroad car designated for African Americans. In its ruling, the court effectively allowed segregation of public spaces, arguing for "separate but equal" resources to be provided to all citizens.

Regents of the University of California v. Bakke This Supreme Court case in 1978 upheld practices by universities to use race as a means of deciding on admission of students.

segregation The process of legal separation of races in public spaces, as established in the United States Supreme Court case *Plessy v. Ferguson*. In the ruling, the court declared "separate but equal" facilities permissible.

social justice Justice in the distribution of wealth, opportunities, and privileges within a society.

solicitor general The deputy law officer to the attorney general for the United States of America. The solicitor general is responsible for representing the United States government in front of the Supreme Court.

Supreme Court of the United States The highest judicial institution in the United States, the Supreme Court exercises supreme legal authority over the nation. The court reviews the actions of other branches of government, hears cases involving federal law, and considers federal appeals of cases decided by lower courts.

Further Information

Books

Aldred, Lisa. *Thurgood Marshall: Supreme Court Justice.* Black Americans of Achievement. New York: Chelsea House Publishers, 2005.

Clack, George, editor. *Justice for All: The Legacy of Thurgood Marshall.* Washington, DC: US Department of State, Bureau of International Information Programs, 2007.

Davis, Michael D. and Hunter R. Clark. *Thurgood Marshall: Warrior at the Bar, Rebel on the Bench.* New York: Birch Lane Press, 1992.

Tushnet, Mark. *Making Constitutional Law: Thurgood Marshall and the Supreme Court, 1961–1991.* New York: Oxford University Press, 1997.

Williams, Juan. *Thurgood Marshall: American Revolutionary.* New York: Three Rivers Press, 1998.

Websites

BlackPast.org
www.blackpast.org

This website is an online reference for African-American history.

Thurgood Marshall: Supreme Court Justice and Civil Rights Advocate
thurgoodmarshall.com

This site was set up to inform people about the man who fought for equal rights for African Americans.

"With an Even Hand": Brown v. Board at Fifty
www.loc.gov/exhibits/brown/brown-segregation.html

The Library of Congress looks at a century of racial discrimination from 1849 to 1950, and provides links to other resources.

Videos

Thurgood Marshall
www.biography.com/people/thurgood-marshall-9400241/videos/thurgood-marshall-full-episode-2192395509

A full-length video on the life of Thurgood Marshall and other content about civil rights can be viewed at this site.

Thurgood Marshall Nominated to Supreme Court
www.youtube.com/watch?v=ri0NwkwkkoE

This video excerpt from the UCLA Film and Television Archive is a news report on the nomination by President Lyndon Baines Johnson of Thurgood Marshall to the Supreme Court.

Thurgood Marshall Videos
www.history.com/topics/black-history/thurgood-marshall/videos

The History Channel provides links to videos involving civil rights events that have a connection to Thurgood Marshall.

Bibliography

Brown, Henry. "*Plessy v. Ferguson.*" May 18, 1896. TeachingAmericanHistory.org. Accessed November 3, 2015. http://teachingamericanhistory.org/library/document/plessy-v-ferguson-excerpts.

"Court of Appeals of Maryland: Pearson, et. al. v. Murray." *Beyond Brown: Pursuing the Promise*. PBS. Accessed November 3, 2015. http://www.pbs.org/beyondbrown/brownpdfs/pearsonmurray.pdf.

Du Bois, W. E. B. "The Talented Tenth." September 1903. Accessed November 3, 2015. TeachingAmericanHistory.org. http://teachingamericanhistory.org/library/document/the-talented-tenth.

Eisenhower, Dwight D. "Mob Rule Cannot Be Allowed to Override the Decisions of Our Courts." History Matters. Accessed November 7, 2015. http://historymatters.gmu.edu/d/6335.

Johnson, Lyndon B. "Remarks to the Press Announcing the Nomination of Thurgood Marshall as Associate Justice of the Supreme Court." June 13, 1967. The American Presidency Project. Accessed November 7, 2015. http://www.presidency.ucsb.edu/ws/?pid=28298.

Lincoln, Abraham. "Letter to Major General Joseph Hooker." January 26, 1863. Abraham Lincoln Online. Accessed November 7, 2015. http://www.abrahamlincolnonline.org/lincoln/speeches/hooker.htm.

Marshall, Thurgood. "Argument Before the US Supreme Court in *Brown v. Board of Education*." 1953. Black Past. Accessed November 7, 2015. http://www.blackpast.org/1953-thurgood-marshall-argument-u-s-supreme-court-brown-v-board-education.

————. "Commentary: Reflections on the Bicentennial of the United States Constitution." *Valapriso University Law Review* 26, no. 1 (1991): 21–25. http://scholar.valpo.edu/vulr/vol26/iss1/8.

————. "Majority Opinion by Thurgood Marshall in *Mempa v. Rhay* (1967)." Taylor & Francis, 2013. Accessed November 7, 2015. http://documents.routledge-interactive.s3.amazonaws.com/9780415506434/document7.pdf.

————. "*Regents of the University of California v. Bakke* Separate Opinion." Legal Information Institute: Cornell University Law School. Accessed November 3, 2015. http://www.law.cornell.edu/supremecourt/text/438/265#writing-USSC_CR_0438_0265_ZX2.

————. *Thurgood Marshall: His Speeches, Writings, Arguments, Opinions, and Reminisces.* Edited by Mark Tushnet. Chicago: Lawrence Hill Books, 2001.

Mann, Jim. "Jurist Was on Front Lines in Anti-Segregation Fight: Profile: As a lawyer and judge, the great-grandson of a slave successfully fought legal obstacles to integration." *Los Angeles Times*, June 28, 1991. http://articles.latimes.com/1991-06-28/news/mn-1286_1_supreme-court.

"University of Maryland v. Donald G. Murray," Thurgood Marshall Law Library: University of Maryland Francis King Carey School of Law. Accessed November 3, 2015. http://www.law.umaryland.edu/marshall/specialcollections/murray/169mdr478.pdf.

Washington, Booker T. "Booker T. Washington Delivers the 1895 Atlanta Compromise Speech." History Matters: The US Survey Course on the Web. Accessed November 3, 2015. http://historymatters.gmu.edu/d/39.

Index

affirmative action, 41–43, **42**

Baltimore, 9–10, **10**, 12, 16, 20

Brown v. Board of Education of Topeka
  constituent cases, 23–24
  decision, 26–27, **28**, 29
  implementation of, 29–31, 33–34, 44
  legacy of, 29, 31, 33, 39, 43, 46–48
  legal arguments, 24–26
  plaintiffs, 25

Clark, Kenneth, 24, 37, 37

Du Bois, W. E. B., 7–8, **8**

Eisenhower, Dwight D., 30–31, 33
Emancipation Proclamation, 52–53, **53**
equality, 5–8, 12–13, 17, 20, 22–23, 26, 31, 39–44, 48–49, 51–52

Faubus, Orval, 29–30, 36, **36**

Fourteenth Amendment, 4–5, 13, 20, 25–26, 39, 41, 46, 51

Houston, Charles Hamilton, 8–9, 11, **16**, 17–20, 22–23, 29
Howard University, 8–9, 11, 13, 18, 22

integration, 8, 10, 23, 33–34, 36, 44–45, **45**

Johnson, Lyndon, 35, 38–39, **38**
judicial opinion, 5, 11, 21, 26–7, **28**, 29, 39, 41–43, 46

Kennedy, John F., 34–35
King, Martin Luther, Jr., 31, 33–34, 39

legal counsel, 8, 14, **14**, 34
Little Rock Nine, 29–30, **32**, 34, **45**
lynching, 11, 17, 35

Marshall, Thurgood
  activism and, 33, 40–41

Thurgood Marshall and *Brown v. Board of Education of Topeka*

Brown v. Board of
Education and, 23–26,
27, 49–50
early life, 9–13
Federal Court of Appeals,
34–35, 52
legal philosophy, 11–13,
17, 46–52
Little Rock Nine and, 30,
32, 34
Murray v. Pearson and,
18–22, 19, 21
NAACP and, 11, 13, **14**,
15–27, 34, 52
private practice, 13–15
solicitor general, 38–39,
38, 46, 52
Supreme Court justice,
39–46, **40**, **50**, 52
Meredith, James, **30**, 31, **47**
Murray, Donald Gaines,
18–22, **19**, **21**
Murray v. Pearson, 18–23, 52

NAACP, 8, **8**, 11, **14**, 15–18,
16, 20, 22–24, 29, 33–35, 52

Plessy v. Ferguson, 5, **6**, 17,
20, 42

**Regents of the University of
California v. Bakke**, 41–43

segregation, 5–11, 10, 17–
18, 22–26, 29, 31, 35–37,
36, **37**, 46–47, 50, 52
social justice, 10
solicitor general, 38–39, **38**,
46, 52
**Supreme Court of the
United States**, 5, **10**, 15,
22–27, **28**, 29–31, **29**, **32**,
35–36, 39, **40**, 41–46,
49–49, **50**, 51–52

Warren, Earl, 26–27, **28**, 29, 33
Washington, Booker T., 7

About the Author

ZACHARY DEIBEL is the Social Studies Department Chair at Marked Tree High School in Marked Tree, Arkansas. A graduate of American University in Washington, DC, he enjoys reading, writing, and thinking about American history. His forthcoming masters thesis considers the diversity of early political ideology in the American Revolutionary and Constitutional periods.

Thurgood Marshall and *Brown v. Board of Education of Topeka*